Signature Woman

Magazine

Many daughters have done well, But you excel them all.

Proverbs 31:29

We Believe

God is the creator of the universe both seen and unseen.

God is the giver of life.

The Trinity – The Father, The Son, The Holy Ghost

The death of Jesus provides complete atonement of our sins.

All of God's Word and stand firm on it knowing that it is the same yesterday, today, and forever.

Jesus rose from the dead and is seated at the right hand of God and we have access to him through prayer and fellowship.

Greater love has no one than this, than to lay down one's life for his friends. – John 15:13

In the beginning was the Word, and the Word was with God, and the Word was God. – John 1:1

Signature Woman
Magazine

Many daughters have done well, But you excel them all.
Proverbs 31:29

Publisher

DeLonda Adams

Contributors

Sean Adams
Rebecca Evans
Myra Jordan
LaQuitea Vaughn
Crystal Miller
Cheryl Meakins
Aretha Turner
Lisa Ellis Williams
Dawn Covin
April Jackson

P.O. BOX 172624 • Denver, CO 80217
www.proverbs31mama.org

Signature Woman
Magazine

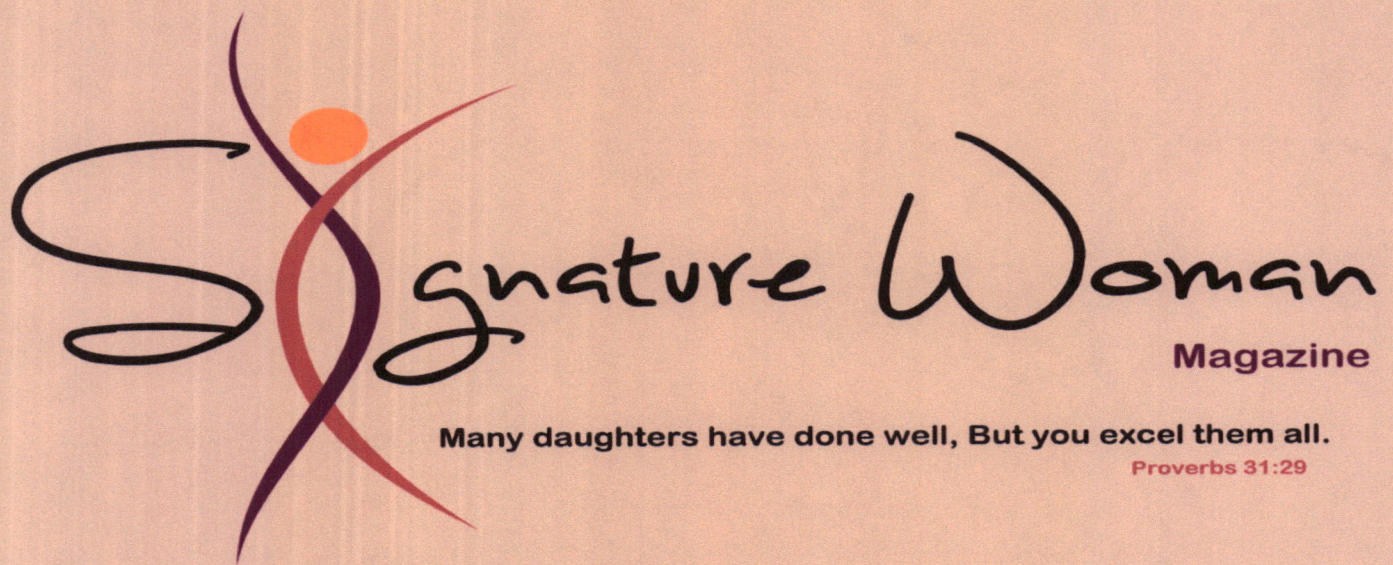

Many daughters have done well, But you excel them all.
Proverbs 31:29

Table of Contents

From the Publisher

Welcome to our Signature Woman Magazine! Proverbs 31 Mama Ministries is growing by leaps and bounds and we are going to continue to give God all the glory in everything we do!

Did you know that God is doing a NEW THING! Yes He is and I pray that you will see with your spiritual eyes all the wonderful and creative things our God is doing. If you are caught up in distractions of what others are doing, what your circumstances are, and how it did not work for you in 2012 this new thing will quickly pass you buy.

I truly believe this year God wants to do something in the body that will make the wise take a second look and scratch their heads. That means that we are going to finally take our hands off of some things and see how the Master unfolds the plan right before our very eyes. Will it be easy? At times no but I promise you the end will be well worth the toil. It has been long enough and the time is now to see what our God can really do for us. No more looking at others and wishing God will do it for us because He can and He will. We only need to take our hands off the wheel and sit at the Father's feet and hear His word and focus on the better thing and watch how the Lord honors you while you honor Him at His feet.

God Bless You

DeLonda Adams

Founder of Proverbs 31 Mama
Creator of Signature Woman

{
Behold, I will do a new thing; now it shall spring forth; shall ye not know it? I will even make a way in the wilderness, *and* rivers in the desert.

Isaiah 43:19
}

It's Tea Time!

Tea Talk with DeLonda

Real & Relevant

Casual talk for the mamas

Join me for some R&R

Real & Relevant Discussions

Every 3rd Tuesday Beginning

March 19, 2013

@ 12:30 PM CST

Visit our site for more details

www.Proverbs31Mama.org

(under the ministry tab)

Love is in the air. Couples are walking hand in hand on chilly nights into nearly overcrowded and expensive restaurants. They are exchanging tokens of love or bemoaning tight budgets. This time of the year the love bug has bitten its fair share of star-crossed lovers and eyes are set ablaze with passion while the hypothalamus is firing off endorphins on all cylinders and a concoction of pheromones and pricy eau de toilettes are being inhaled. Yes it is truly a magnificent time; Valentines, a day for lovers to celebrate and affirm their love.

Love biblically is sorted into 3 different types: *agape*, *phileo*, and *storge*. Of course societally we would be remiss if we didn't mention *eros*, which is the main type of love we see purported in erotica or pornography. While erotica is a multi-billion dollar industry it is still a very cheap and twisted play on real love and its expressions. The term *eros* is not in the Bible, it is simply a Greek word for love, but if Paul had used a word for love when discussing people getting married so that they don't burn with passion, he might have chosen *eros*, because it is carnal (1 Corinthians 7:9). Carnality is not an evil taboo, in this term, carnal simply means of the flesh or self.

As Christians our hope is that we can take our carnal based passions and hone them to be focused solely on one mate and not shared willy-nilly with whomever we fancy. So we enter marriage; a sacred covenant which consecrates our passions and binds them to one person. When we marry, two persons become one and this physical act which is simultaneously spiritual; testifies of Christ (Ephesians 5:31-33). Something happens when we do this. Our *eros* type love has the opportunity to be submitted to God and blessed, therein changing it to an *agape* type love.

Imagine a couple passing two huge medicine balls back and forth. The balls will start to feel heavy after a while and the couple may tire, those balls are an example of *eros* type love, it is their own love, in their own strength, being passed between them on their own individual terms. Continuing with our imagination God enters the mix via marriage and the couple places their individual huge medicine balls of love in the permanent care of God and their spouse. They then are given very light tennis balls to pass between each other, and the juggle starts, but is far less taxing. You see God's burden is easy and yoke is light, even His love. Now the couple is not passing their own love and expectations between themselves, they are passing God's *agape* amongst themselves. His *agape* is an all forgiving, unconditional, tried and true love; it won't fail even if man does (1 Corinthians 13). This is the upgrade of marriage or at least it should be.

Could you imagine if all Christian couples loved this way, could you imagine the way our families would look, our communities and our nation if the family loved each other with agape love. What if you did it? What would change? Would you be happier if you stopped holding your list of failed expectations over your spouse's head, or if your spouse lost their list of the insurmountable expectations they are burdening the relationship with? Can you only imagine? Give it a try. I am convinced that if the love between the husband and wife is becoming too taxing, they are juggling the wrong balls.

Pastor Sean L. Adams
Epiphany Covenant Church

4

Help Me Heal!
6 Ways to mend from childhood abuse

By: Cheryl Meakins

Childhood abuse has a way of permeating your soul, infecting your mind, and sabotaging your faith. And when you least expect it, the effects of that abuse insert themselves into healthy situations, mucking up your everyday life. At least that's what it did to me.

I was five years old when it happened but I was forty when I remembered. And that was the sexual abuse. All the other kinds of abuse I remembered all too well. Package all the abuse into the premise of a Christian home and it really got confusing!

Unfortunately, I have a common story. Fortunately, God knows how to heal.

Abuse holds power way beyond the incident, imprinting lies into our souls causing us to act out of our fears. Healing is the process of stripping abuse of its power, the power it wields in two ways.

First abuse mars the image of God. Because God is love, the warping of love changes who we believe God to be. This breach of trust stands in the way of us seeking the one relationship that can heal us.

To heal we must ask God to rebuild who he is.

My healing began when I prayed a bold prayer.
"God who-you-say-you-are in your word, and who-I-see-in-my-life, doesn't match up. I know you say you are good, but I just don't see the good in my life. So today I'm throwing everything out, the good with the bad, and I start with what I do know to be true. You are God the Father who sent his son Jesus Christ to live and die for my sins. He is alive today and I am forgiven. Other than that I'm a blank slate. Start over with me."

Meditate on Hosea 2
– When reading Hosea my attention was drawn to God's attitude towards Gomer.

Gomer was a woman left vulnerable to the abusive occupation of prostitution. Even when Gomer was offered a way out of abuse and into unconditional love with Hosea she could not make herself stay.

After a whole chapter of reprimand, jealousy and anger, God changes the story and chapter 2 reveals his tender heart towards a woman wounded so deeply she was afraid to trust love. If you read these words through the eyes of an abused woman you might get a glimpse of how great God's love is toward those of us that have been sexually abused.

Create - When abuse damages the image of God, it also damages our self-image because we were made in His image.

LeAnne Payne, in her book Restoring the Christian Soul, talks about how we are made in the image of The Creator. Of all God's creation, we are distinctly different in that we can also create. When we create we are connecting with our Creator.

You may have a creative outlet or need to explore your own creativity. Keep doing it! Creativity showed me how to walk out of mourning and into dancing. Do not diminish the importance of creative space in your life.

Secondly abuse transfers guilt from the perpetrator to the victim and does so through a *system* of abuse propagated by the family. The victim lives with guilt under the name of Shame. Shame wields the power to keep a secret. Bringing the secret into the light within a safe community is the key.

Find a Counselor – I can't emphasize enough the importance of skilled care for your soul. You will need to find a counselor who supports the important piece of understanding the heart of God toward you. Your therapist should also be trained in working with abuse victims, and PTSD (post-traumatic stress disorder). My counselor uses a technique called EMDR (eye movement and desensitization reprocessing) to help move the traumatic memories of abuse out of the fight or flight area of my brain and into the cortex. It is a method of therapy I strongly recommend.

Read Mending the Soul. This is one of the most comprehensive Christian books on healing from abuse. Stephen Tracy, the author, and his wife Celestia lead the ministry of Mending the Soul. You can find out more about their ministry and small group training at www.MendingtheSoul.org

It takes a great deal of courage to heal!

Give yourself permission to cry, wrestle, mourn, and be angry, for out of that process will come days of laughter, joy and dancing. Let each day be what it is, you can keep going, knowing that everyday is filled with Christ.

Cheryl is passionate to see whole women wholly serving God. After returning to her first love of writing four years ago and embarking on speaking and teaching she has found her calling: To walk with women into freedom who are healing from abuse; childhood, domestic abuse as well as confronting the evil of human trafficking. She has recently been published as a contributing author to two devotional books. "If I can do all things through Christ, Why can't I find my car keys" and "Big Dreams from Small Spaces" by Group Publishing. You can visit her ministry and blog at www.MeakinsSpeak.com

Ministry Moments ♥

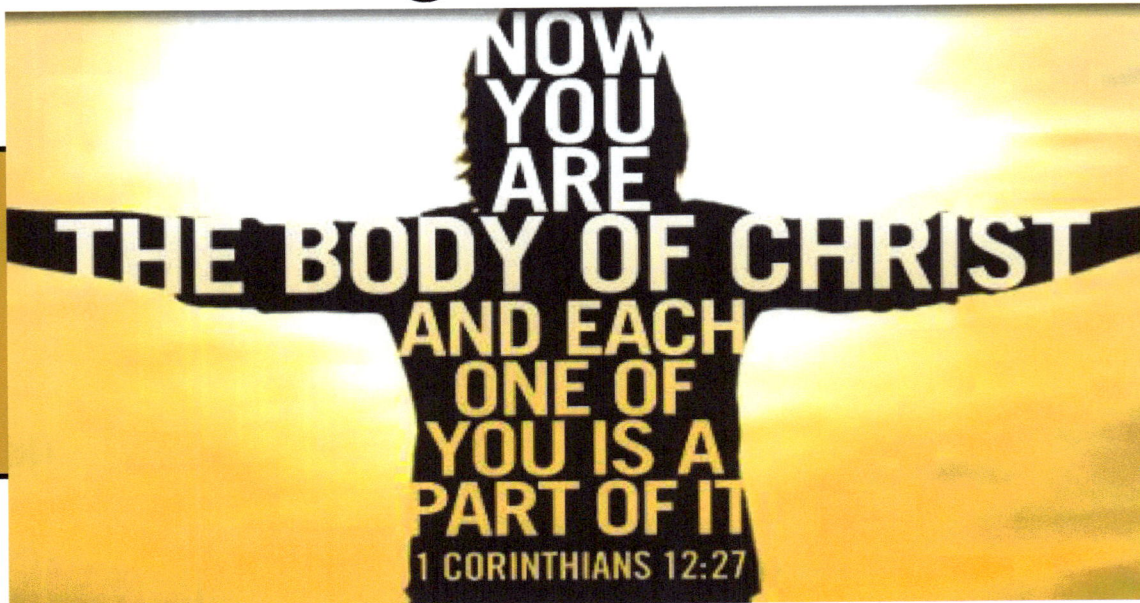

NOW YOU ARE THE BODY OF CHRIST AND EACH ONE OF YOU IS A PART OF IT
1 CORINTHIANS 12:27

WE ARE ONE IN CHRIST JESUS

(No room for competition)

We are God's family, one in Christ Jesus! *"For just as each of us has one body with many members, and these members do not all have the same function, so in Christ we, though many, form one body, and each member belongs to all the others."* Romans 12:4-5

If we are one, in the body of Christ and we belong to each other then why in the kingdom of God do we compete with one another? (strive to outdo another for acknowledgment, a prize, supremacy, profit, etc.) I think the answer to that question lies in the motive of why we do what we do and requires an individual heart check. Are you about self-glorification or God-Exaltation? All glory belongs to God and Him along.

"So whether you eat or drink or whatever you do, do it all for the glory of God." 1 Corinthians 10:31

By Myra Jordan

Looking unto Jesus

the author and finisher of our faith; who for the joy that was set before Him endured the cross, despising the shame, and is set down at the right hand at the throne of God.

Hebrews 12:2

with *Rebecca Evans*

The Love of a Father

God is the very essence of Love. He is love. That is God's nature. As we reflect on His agape love for us, we do not have to rely on words like, "I Love you" rather He showed his love to us through action. We all know the bible verse John 3:16, it has been rehearsed in our minds over and over again. Most of us have this bible verse memorized and it truly is a powerful verse. But do you believe it? "For God so loved the world, that he gave his only begotten Son, that whosoever believeth in him should not perish, but have everlasting life." If you are someone who lost touch with love because of abandonment or someone abusing the word love in your life don't ever feel like you are not loved because God's love for you is greater than anyone else on this earth. He loves the lovely and unlovely parts of us. But you must know God who loves us sent His Son to pay the price so that we could be saved from the punishment we all justly deserve. God demonstrates his own love toward us, in that while we were yet sinners, Christ died for us." Romans 5:8 Jesus sacrificed Himself for the sins of the world. That is a powerful real love, crazy love, supernatural love and those words we need to integrate deep into our being.

There is nothing that can come between God's love for you. We are created in His image. His very hand formed and made you. He knows no limits and may you have the power to understand, as all God's people should, how wide, how long, how high, and how deep His love is. Ephesians 3:18. We love Him because he first loved us (1 John 4:19) and because God's love toward us, we are now able to love one another. See how great a love the Father has bestowed on us, that we would be called children of God; and such we are. 1 John 3:1. You are greatly loved and cherished by a loving and holy God! Trust God that His love for you is the greatest, you are worthy of everlasting life through Jesus Christ!

Looking Unto Jesus,
Rebecca

What great love the father has lavished on us!

John 3:1

love revealed

8

Hand Me Downs

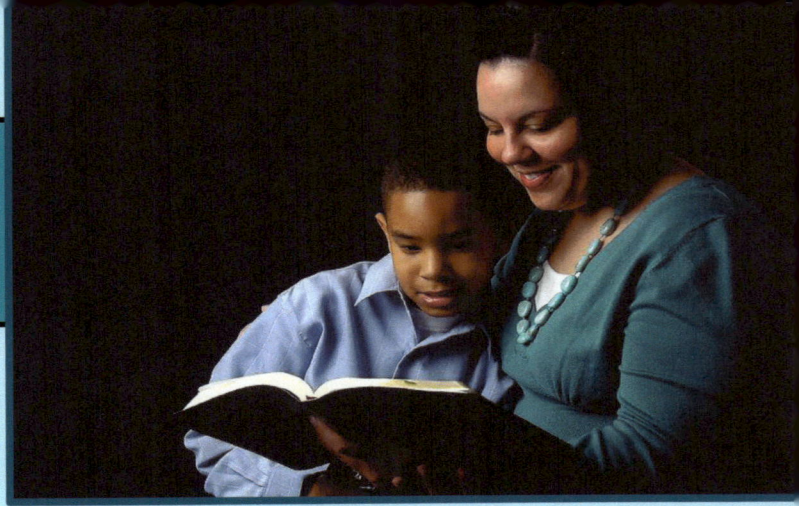

I know a lot about passing things down. What I like to call hand-me-downs, a fun verb that has been transformed into a noun over the decades. I grew up on these things and would get downright giddy when I received a black trash bag full of the things. Basically, hand-me-downs are used clothes passed to a sibling, cousin, or even a family friend to get the most use out of them while saving money. I too am carrying the torch by saving my oldest daughters clothes for my baby girl.

Some people look down on used things, but not me. It's all in your thinking. Even as a girl, I would take used garments and pair them with different pieces of mine to make them special and unique to me. All the while knowing my wonderful creation wouldn't look like anyone else. Some outfits were a flop and some were successful, but in my mind I was a fashion designer.

So, do you take hand-me-downs for your children? What are your children receiving clothes, shoes, accessories? If so, that is great, but there is even more.

2 Timothy 1:5 MSG

That precious memory triggers another: your <u>honest faith</u>—and what a <u>rich faith</u> it is, handed down from your grandmother Lois to your mother Eunice, and now to you!

In this verse, Paul is writing a letter to Timothy. Through the reading, Paul's excitement and appreciation for "hand-me-downs" is plainly seen. Beginning at verse 5, Paul begins to speak of Timothy's faith. In the Message Bible he describes it as honest and rich.

What a powerful statement! I would love nothing more than for others to describe my faith as honest and rich. The second part of that scripture describes the origin of Timothy's honest and rich faith.

After reading the lineage of Timothy's faith beginning with Grandma Lois, to mother Eunice, and then on to Timothy, I was struck. What am I handing down? What do my girls have to show for living and being raised by me? What are my grandchildren going to have to show for my faith? Is it an honest and rich faith or doubt and unbelief?

Every day that passes, I've handed down a little more. The most striking thing about this thought is it's not an optional action. I will hand down something – not just clothes and toys, but my faith (or lack of) be it honest and rich or sorry and slack. The choice is completely up to me!

By: Crystal Miller
[Able to See](#)

Right There in Black & White

By Lisa Ellis Williams

The month of February ushers in a few unique celebrations. Ground Hog's day sparks attention on the morning news as the little rodent from Punxsutawney, PA looks for his shadow thereby making a prediction about when Spring will come. Black History week has evolved into a month long parade of posters, programs and library books strategically presented to convey the significant accomplishments by African Americans in the United States. Then there is Valentine's Day when red and pink stuffed bears, balloons, and expensive boxes of candy emerge displaying love notes addressed to a sweetheart.

Valentine's Day products are sold in commercial stores, specialty boutiques and even street side venders stirring fantasy and evoking romantic images in even the teenage mind. Women who want to be married frequently generate excitement with public displays of affection while married women sit idly by watching provocative behavior portrayed in scenes on TV or in novels. For many wives, Valentine's Day can be one of the most disappointing days of the year. If you can relate, the answer is right there in front of you.

Black and White

Instead of hot red and bright pink, determine this year that your love line will be drawn by the black and white. Here it is. The Bible tells us in Hebrews 13:4a **"Marriage should be honored by all, and the marriage bed kept pure."** God gives permission to honor your marriage in the bed and to keep it pure. Since marriages go through four seasons, I have put together this list of creative ways to honor your marriage on Valentine's Day in every season. Note actions, motives, and expectations are different in every season.

Valentine's Day Tips for every season of marriage

Summer: You and Your husband are on fire for one another

➢ Buy or make a card that describes your tingly feelings for your husband.
➢ Dress in the outfit you know he likes.
➢ Plan to stay up late on February 14th, play romantic music, and kiss his body until you have touched every pimple, scar, and mole.
➢ Tell him why you love him.

Fall: Things seem different and you sense some distance creeping in

➢ Buy or make a card that clearly defines what your husband represents in your life.
➢ Take special notice of your outward appearance. Dress in modest clothes during the day and sexy ones at night.
➢ Play music that you and your husband enjoy.

➢ On February 14th initiate intimacy. Remind him how much you desire him and give him what **he** wants.

Winter: You and your husband live together comfortably doing your own thing or you are separated

➢ Write a letter telling God your true feelings about your husband. Once you are done destroy it. Your complaints are for you and God only.
➢ Buy a card that acknowledges your marriage. "To my husband, Happy Valentine's Day" is sufficient. Mail it to him even if you live together. Wait until he tells you that he received it. If he doesn't then don't' ask. You are choosing to obey God and honor your marriage.
➢ Dress in clothes that make you feel and look cute. They should fit properly and reflect your personal style. Your husband will notice when you take pride in your appearance even if he doesn't admit it.
➢ Play praise music in your home constantly and turn off any romantic songs. They will only hurt your feelings.
➢ Plan for February 14th by being quiet. Refrain from making any demands or dropping subtle reminders to your husband about Valentine's Day. He did not forget.
➢ Guard your heart from disappointment by investing in a happy wife. Purchase a gift card for her to celebrate Valentine's Day with her husband

Spring: You and your husband have gotten over the hurt. New love is budding while you are learning to fully trust again.

➢ Write a letter expressing your commitment to your husband. Let him know why you are still with him.
➢ Dress pretty all of the time. It will make both of you take a second look at the women you have become. You are growing in beauty and godliness.
➢ Play praise music during the day and romantic music at night. It will keep your feelings fresh.
➢ Plan something fun to do on Valentine's Day. One activity that you share is perfect. If you don't have much in common any more then pick one of his favorites.
➢ Increase romance by increasing frequency. More is often better in the Spring time.

My marriage has thrived after twenty four years because I have used God's word to lead me through every season. It's right there in black and white. This Valentine's Day, I invite you to **celebrate no matter what season you are in.** Pick up all that is hot red and pink if you like but, remember you are married. That is why you celebrate a day of love.

Godly wives honor marriage on purpose. It's right there, in black and white. Happy Valentine's Day!

Lisa Ellis Williams, writer, speaker, and creator of Wives On Purpose ministry. Since 2004 Lisa has taught hundreds of women to apply biblical principles for marriage in practical ways. Her strong faith and deep passion touches the hearts of women, igniting a desire to stay married. Lisa equips women with the skills necessary to maintain healthy marriages, build strong families, serve broader communities, and impact the world. Sign up for her free newsletter and find out more about Lisa's work at
www.wivesonpurposeministry.com

Celebrate the Season

I know it may not feel like it where you live, but Spring is just around the corner (I hope). With the change of season comes the need to shake off the winter blues and for some of us that may mean dinner parties, Sunday brunches, and outdoor gatherings. So, how can we celebrate the season? That's easy: take a cue from nature.

One of the easiest ways to bring a breath of fresh spring air into your celebrations is by using lots of fresh, vibrant colors. One of my favorite color combinations is pink and tangerine, but you can also use colors like yellow, green, and blue to enhance your décor. Of course nothing says spring like flowers so use lots of fresh flowers. If it's a ladies only event, then you may even consider giving each of your guests a small corsage. To do this without blowing your budget use carnations. Carnations are pretty, inexpensive, and available at most local grocery stores. Trust me ladies, these flowers have come a long way from the days of prom.

Do you or any of your guests suffer from seasonal allergies? No need to worry. Fresh fruit, whole or sliced, is just as gorgeous and classy as fresh flowers. Try stacking lemons and limes in a bowl, tall vase, or even an overturned cake dome. For a super chic twist combine the fruit and flowers. Think lilies and limes.

Well, if you don't have any spring events on your social calendar, I hope I have inspired you to add one (or a few) so that you can celebrate the season.

LaQuitea Vaughn
Visions by Vaughn

12

The Proverbs 31 Woman

She is the most rare gem.
She walks with confidence before them.
She lacks nothing all her days.
And goodness is what she rays.

She works with a servant's heart.
Decisions she makes are always smart.
Her light is always on to shine before men.
To those in need and poverty, her hand, she lends.

Her household is covered with her love.
She is one sent from above.
She picks a man who sits among the wise,
Her profits are always the right size.

Strength is at her heart's core.
Her laughter is the most adored.
Words of Christ are out of her mouth.
Her actions are never in doubt.

She is productive as a woman should be.
She is blessed, do you see?
All of the noble, she surpasses.
Like David, she always dances.

She is more than beauty, more than charm.
Her praise of God is in lifted arms.
Her rewards are in the Heaven's gate.
To catch her, true love of Jesus is your bait.

By: Lydia Marisela Mena

Why I Homeschool When "I Don't Wanna"
By Dawn Covin

Almost every mother can relate to the often times whining phrase 'I don't wanna!" Whether it is about putting on shoes, cleaning up toys, or going to bed, I am sure you have at least heard it once. At some point, our children grow and mature and our communication process with them improves, and they often begin to see that we are truly looking out for the best interests, with the goal of raising them with the best foundation for the future.

As I enter the second half of my sixth year of homeschooling, I know that I have had the "I don't wanna" thoughts often. My husband and I have four daughters (yes, FOUR girls, ages 11, 9, 7, and 2) and the days are sometimes filled with tattling, bickering, and a house that can never stay clean. Add to these frustrations the anxiety of making sure your children are 'on track' and suddenly, the idea of homeschooling doesn't seem all that appealing. People go to school and get paid to do this, why should I do it? That yellow school bus starts to look better and better every day.

"But God", is a phrase that we see often in the Bible that follows acts that initially seem unsalvageable. My convictions regarding God's place in the life of our children is what is at the core of my reasons for homeschooling. I have decided to not allow my momentary weaknesses and irritability of my flesh to separate me from the Lord's commands. As my prayer life and discipleship continue to mature, I see evidence that God is at work in the hearts of our entire family through the 'togetherness' of homeschooling. I am training myself to look beyond today's inconveniences and keep in sight the big picture, the main objective, which is so clearly stated in Deuteronomy 6. When I start feeling the "I don't wannas", I'm reminded of these commands and I take my head from under my covers and trust that God is with me and that potty training and teaching long division at the same time will NOT last forever.

Deuteronomy 6: 5-9
New Living Translation (NLT)

And you must love the Lord your God with all your heart, all your soul, and all your strength. And you must commit yourselves wholeheartedly to these commands that I am giving you today. Repeat them again and again to your children. Talk about them when you are at home and when you are on the road, when you are going to bed and when you are getting up. Tie them to your hands and wear them on your forehead as reminders. Write them on the doorposts of your house and on your gates.

Saying No to the Status Quo
www.offdachainandouttadabox.wordpress.com

Proverbs 31 Mama Covenant

I will keep my Lord & Savior Jesus Christ first and will seek Him above all things.

I will not lose my identity in the things of this world. My identity is in Christ alone.

With God's grace I will be a woman who walks after the spirit and not in the flesh so that I can be the wife that does good and not evil all the days of her life.

I will be a good steward over the resources that God blesses my home with.

I will not sit on the gifts and talents that the Lord has blessed me with. Rather I will walk out my purpose with those gifts and talents for the glory of God.

I will not give myself over to idle things that do not glorify
God or encourage me in my walk with Him.

I will do whatever is possible to make it easier for my
husband to walk out the call of God on His life.

I will not leave it up to the schools, church, friends, or relatives to teach my child. I will take the responsibility to train up my child in the things of the Lord seriously.

I will not only focus on my world but I will stretch out my hand to help others in need. I will not complain about what I do not have to give because
God has blessed me with something to give.

I will not boast about all that I do but rather I will let my works speak for me. As my works praise me at the gates I will be praising God for His grace through it all.

If I fall in any of these areas I will get up and try again.

Proverbs 31 Mama

Fitness In the New Year!

By: April Jackson of Sweat Everyday

Your body should prosper just as your mind and your spirit does. You exercise your spirit by reading the bible, attending bible study, praying, going to church, and fellow shipping with others. You exercise your mind by reading newspapers, blogs, books, watching the news and staying current on recent events. How do you keep your physical body fit? Do you eat healthy, well balanced meals, exercise, and maintain doctors' appointments for yourself?

Oftentimes, as women, we make sure everyone else is taken care of. We make all of our family members eat right, get involved in physical activities and, make their doctors' appointments. It is important that we as women make sure that we take care ourselves. In order to take care of others we have to be of sound mind and body. The focus here is our body. Being healthy and fit is so important.

It is vitally important that we, as women, take our fitness into account in the New Year. I KNOW finding the time to do so when you work outside or inside the home is challenging BUT it can be done. I suggest you "take five" for yourself.

1) Make sure you have all of your scheduled doctors' visits this year (dentist, gynecology, physical). Staying informed and checked up is important to your fitness.

2) If you cannot find the time or resources to workout in a gym or take classes, just workout at home. There are many programs on TV, Video on demand and Apps on your phone for free! You can even access DVD's at your local library.

3) EAT RIGHT!! Cook well balanced meals. Try to stay away from fast food as much as you can. Only buy healthy foods to snack on and cook in your home. Don't feel guilty about treating yourself to dessert or a snack.
Just remember moderation and the 80/20 rule. 80 percent of what your fitness goals should be healthy eating.

4) Have support! Who do you fellowship with? Are they active? Do they have a healthy lifestyle and can they encourage you? Get connected with someone who will support you in your goals.

5) Try something new and different. Have you considered riding your bike, walking, jogging, running, ZUMBA, rock climbing? Maybe go to the park with your family or friends and play a game. Try something different and see how you like it. Switch up your routines so you stay engaged in your fitness routine.

This isn't a lot and, if you take five minutes a day to think about how you can work on your fitness in the New Year it will accumulate into 1825 minutes in a year! That's approximately 76 days!! WOW! That would really take your fitness up a notch in the New Year!

Working on your fitness this year doesn't need to be an overwhelming, monumental task. A little each day goes a long way. Let your five minute thoughts develop into actions and you will see fitness results in the New Year!

Spring Cleaning

Spring is a time of renewal. The flowers are starting to bloom. I'm sure you are aware, that typically when the seasons change, the weather changes along with the mindset.

When you hear the words spring cleaning, your initial thoughts are normally clearing your house of unwanted items (clutter). Sometimes you may even want to do away with some items just so you can bring in some new things. Most of all, you want your house to be in pristine condition so you do a deep cleaning. We can apply the same concept to our spiritual lives.

So, the first thing is to begin with you.

Don't you realize that all of you together are the temple of God and that the Spirit of God lives in you? God will destroy anyone who destroys this temple. For God's temple is holy, and you are that temple.
1 Corinthians 3:16-17 (NLT)

We want to go through the house and get it spick and span and make sure everything is dusted and made up nicely. Well what about our spiritual life? Things may appear to be polished and organized on the outside.

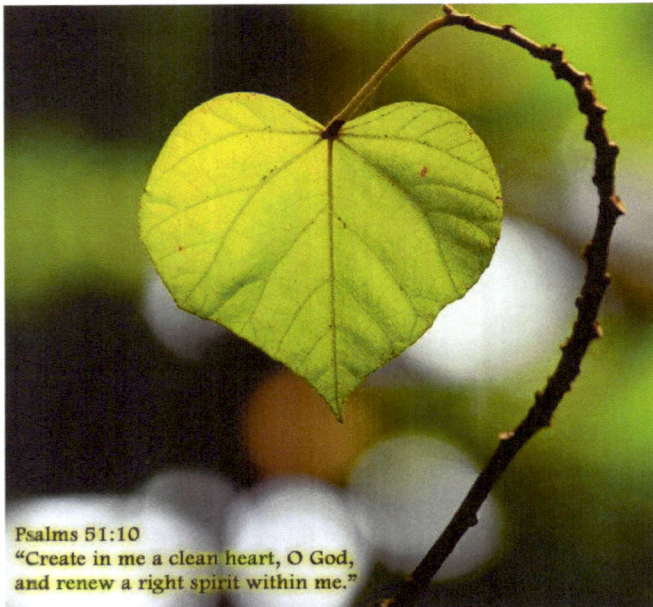

Psalms 51:10
"Create in me a clean heart, O God, and renew a right spirit within me."

However on the exterior, are there areas in your life that need to be pulled away from the wall and inspected?

How is your personal relationship with God? As a wife, you are commissioned to set a godly example of Christian living for your husband as well as your children. This would consist of living a life bringing glory to the Lord. Your relationship with Christ is extremely important. Therefore, you will need to eliminate all distractions that may be hindering your time of intimacy with God. Remember, spring cleaning comes during a season but your spiritual cleaning is eternal.

Create in me a clean heart, O God; and renew a right spirit within me. Psalm 51:10 (KJV)

Your mental capacity could also be cluttered which could hinder your thought process. This could be compared to an attic and we know an attic is used for storage. Since this space is not used often, it becomes really dusty and gloomy. Well when you let things of the past, harmful beliefs, etc. hinder you from the future you are just like the attic. Your state of mind is not functioning up to its full potential. Your thoughts are very powerful. Replace all of the negative thoughts with something positive that exhibit biblical truth. You must believe in the power of the Holy Spirit. Trust and believe God can heal you from all the past hurts, harmful thoughts and negative opinions.

Casting down imaginations, and every high thing that exalteth itself against the knowledge of God, and bringing into captivity every thought to the obedience of Christ. 2 Corinthians 10:5 (KJV)

Sometimes we may have some emotional clutter that may need some disinfectant to scrub away the dirt and grime. Are you having trouble with forgiveness? Maybe you are harboring bitterness or anger in your heart. It's time to let go of the grudges so you can move on in the things God has for you to do. You will not be forgiven if you do not forgive others. You must be free to set an example for others.

Get rid of all bitterness, rage, anger, harsh words, and slander, as well as all types of evil behavior. Instead, be kind to each other, tenderhearted, forgiving one another, just as God through Christ has forgiven you. Ephesians 4:31-32 (NLT)

You must be careful of the words that come from your lips. Once they are out, you are unable to take them back. Do you watch T.V. shows or listen to music that doesn't agree with your spirit? You may have some other form of bad habit. Pray and ask God to help you to clean up your behavior He can and will empower you to resist and overcome the temptation.

A good man out of the good treasure of his heart brings forth good; and an evil man out of the evil treasure of his heart brings forth evil. For out of the abundance of the heart his mouth speaks. Luke 6:45 (NKJ)

Our Heavenly Father is more than capable of freeing us from our sins and unhealthy habits that have accumulated over time. Have faith in Him and He will see you through safely.

Lastly!

Don't you realize that your body is the temple of the Holy Spirit, who lives in you and was given to you by God? You do not belong to yourself, for God bought you with a high price. So you must honor God with your body. 1 Corinthians 6:19-20 (NLT)

"It's time to get rid of the things that are holding you back. Begin today declaring you are going to be a BETTER YOU!"

Now you can have a clean house and a clean soul. ☺

Only by Grace,
Aretha Turner
A Wife's Heart

Times of Refreshing 2013

Repent therefore and be converted, that your sins may be blotted out, so that times of refreshing may come from the presence of the Lord.
Acts 3:19

Proverbs 31 Mama

1st Bi-Annual Retreat

JUNE 20-23, 2013

Westminster, Colorado

THE WESTIN
WESTMINSTER

WORKSHOP SPEAKERS

DeLonda Adams
Denver, CO

Cheryl Meakins
Arvada, CO

ENJOY

Luxury accommodation and amenities

Anointed life changing workshops

Fellowship with your sisters in Christ
♥

Register to Attend
Apply for Sponsorship
Become a Sponsor

For full details on hotel rates and registration visit:

www.proverbs31mama.org

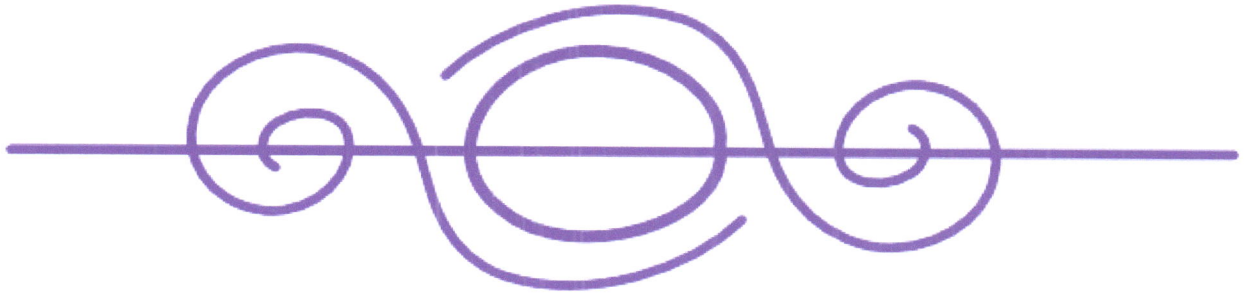

Our Next Signature Woman Issue

Summer 2013

Want to Contribute?

Email us at

contact@proverbs31mama.org

STAY TUNED

Because it will only get better!

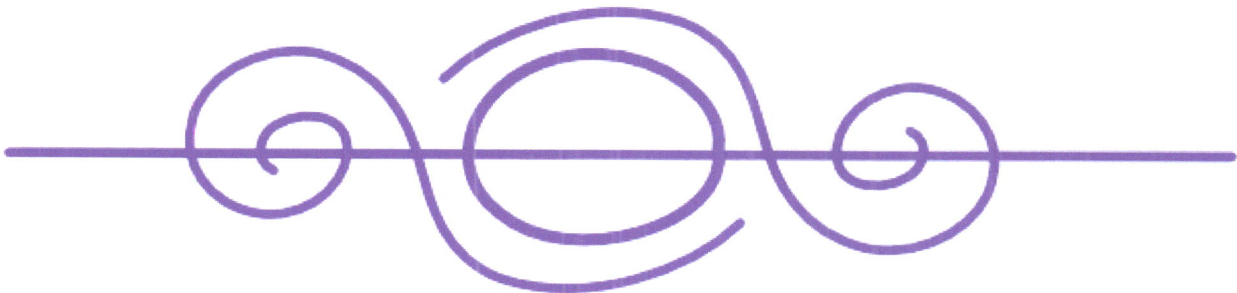

www.ingramcontent.com/pod-product-compliance
Lightning Source LLC
Chambersburg PA
CBHW042120040426
42449CB00002B/124